Tipton Poetry Journal
Editor

Tipton Poetry Journal, located in the heartland of the Midwest, publishes quality poetry from Indiana and around the world.

This issue features 43 poets from the United States (21 different states) and 5 poets from Australia, China, Germany, Italy and Spain.

Review: *Creation Story* by Steven Owen Shields reviewed by Barry Harris

Cover Photo: "Light, Snow" by David Artis

Print versions of *Tipton Poetry Journal* are available for purchase through amazon.com.

Barry Harris, Editor

Copyright 2020 by the Tipton Poetry Journal.

All rights remain the exclusive property of the individual contributors and may not be used without their permission.

Tipton Poetry Journal is published by Brick Street Poetry Inc., a tax-exempt non-profit organization under IRS Code 501(c)(3). Brick Street Poetry Inc. publishes the Tipton Poetry Journal, hosts the monthly poetry series *Poetry on Brick Street* and sponsors other poetry-related events.

Contents

Jiaxin Hao 1

Holly Day 2

Tia Paul-Louis 4

Roy Bentley 6

Joan Colby 8

Matthew Brennan 10

William Greenway 12

Mark Weinrich 13

Jiahui Wu 14

A.C. Shields 16

Erinn Batykefer 17

Bruce Levine 18

Hollie Dugas 18

Carol Hamilton 20

Abbie Hart 21

Michael Jones 22

George Korolog 23

Karla Linn Merrifield 24

Michael Keshigian 24

Gerard Sarnat 26

William Heath 27

Dave Malone 28

Casey Elizabeth Newbegin 30

David Spicer 31

Thomas Alan Orr 32

Patrick Kalahar 33

Michael H. Brownstein 34

Richard Stuecker	*35*
Gaby Bedetti	*36*
Don Kunz	*37*
Katherine Hoerth	*38*
Robert Hirschfield	*39*
Lou Ella Hickman	*41*
Lee Passarella	*42*
Mike Nierste	*43*
Mark Jackley	*44*
Cliff Saunders	*45*
Ellie Dexter	*46*
Cary Barney	*47*
Jenny Kalahar	*48*
Eugene Goldin	*50*
Alessio Zanelli	*51*
John F. Buckley	*52*
John D. Groppe	*54*
Jeanine Stevens	*55*
Simon Perchik	*56*
LuAnne Holladay	*57*
Tyrel Kessinger	*58*
Review: Creation Story by Steven Owen Shields	*59*
Contributor Biographies	*64*

Houses
Jiaxin Hao

Between your house and mine, our parents speak
    Of growing pale as snow and stale as grass
Before the lawn was mown, and things with thorns

Removed, or made into cheap fun to store. We feed
    Like flowers on the dust trail floating by
Like ghosts and neighbors, we moan but cannot fly.

Eventually, we down the blessings of a small town,
Touch frosted lips, whispering of winters,
And endless miles between your house and mine.

Jiaxin Hao is a high school senior in Beijing with a passion for writing. Her poetry has appeared in *Inkbeat Literary Journal* and *Bridge Ink*. She was a finalist for *The New York Times* editorial contest in 2019.

The Little Rabbit
Holly Day

I saw the little rabbit when I was taking the trash out
to the communal apartment dumpster
lying in the middle of the drive on its side, chest moving up and down
a little wet, red bubble forming in one nostril. Someone had hit the rabbit just right
just enough to break its neck or its back but not dead-on, not enough to flatten it
or kill it outright. I put the kitchen garbage in the dumpster and went over to the rabbit
knelt down beside it, saw it tracking me with its wild, wide open eyes.

In every movie I've ever seen, every story I've read
you're supposed to put injured animals
out of their misery, but it just never seemed right to me.
How much is too much for an animal? And if they're so close to the end,
like this tiny brown rabbit was
what if they want every last minute they're allotted? Who am I to steal those
last, precious moments from it?

Carefully, I slipped my hands under its warm little body, felt its heart
beating so fast against my palm, took it over to the side of the driveway
set it down beneath a hedge, somewhere it could feel soft grass and dirt
one last time, instead of the hard, rough asphalt
that smelled of oil and garbage. I thought if the rabbit was going to die anyway
it might as well die somewhere sweet and soft. It squeaked a little when I set it down
I probably hurt it, I hope I didn't .

I don't know why, but a few weeks later
when I was filling out an application form for a job I really wanted to get
when they asked me about something I'd recently done
that I'd been particularly proud of, like some kind of award or achievement.
all I could think about was that rabbit, and how I really felt good
that I'd moved it from the driveway to the grass to die.
I wrote a few lines about the experience, which turned into something
that wrapped around the bottom of the page
and needed to finish somewhere near the middle of the blank back side.
I guess I shouldn't have been surprised
that I never got called back for an interview
but I'm not very good at filling out those things anyway.

A Place and a Thing
Holly Day

They send to the boy to the top of the mountain to think about what he has done.
It's just something that we do, this is what you do
when something needs to be fixed. There are boxes of birds
with their wings broken, eyes sunk into skulls
still covered with bright blue feathers
harbingers of spring, silenced. This silence is something to think about.

The boy sits on the mountaintop, hands figuratively bound,
thoughts metaphorically bound.
There are birds and flowers everywhere here, but they are not his to touch.
He can smell the flowers on the wind
the smell of wheatgrass baking in the sun, the
birds flopping in the undergrowth. They are not his to touch,
he's been told that they never were.
The world is full of souvenirs of conquest
but you can't get caught collecting them.

Holly Day's poetry has recently appeared in Asimov's Science Fiction, Grain, and The Tampa Review. Her newest poetry collections are In This Place, She Is Her Own (Vegetarian Alcoholic Press), A Wall to Protect Your Eyes (Pski's Porch Publishing), Folios of Dried Flowers and Pressed Birds (Cyberwit.net), Where We Went Wrong (Clare Songbirds Publishing), Into the Cracks (Golden Antelope Press), and Cross Referencing a Book of Summer (Silver Bow Publishing).
Holly lives in Minneapolis.

I Was a Bird
Tia Paul-Louis

I danced on branches
where I watched the hill tops
bow down
unforgiven. So they're forgotten.

I saw
where flames pretend
to disappear and how
wind mystifies waters.

I watched prayers ascend.
Some thrown. Some carried,
and I know where spirits live.
Neither high nor below.

I danced on branches safe
and still like

a gentle rescue.

I miss my maple castle.

I now walk—my feet deep
in the grounds like roots running
everywhere. I still fall. Light
fears me. Like an alien before
its time. I beg one eye
to see me. If only I could
rise enough to bow

unforgiven
for what I appear to be
and dare live, I'd
keep living.

Birthmark
Tia Paul-Louis

Three-dimensional spot, opened like a tiny magnolia;
showing edges
with an accent her sight envied and her brows
thrived to reach. A Wow-fit for a tight skin
browned with age, light in despair.
It boasted: 'Birth is engaged.' Diamond uninvited.

Two hands and a knife took it and she welcomed them,
with sleep and compensation.

Now, the mirror shapes a figure she doesn't understand.
She wonders about her name; anxious to give it up
but no record will keep it.

If she could find the bag or can that keeps
that speckle, she'd take it back. But what
returns to her—like a pinch—are
reflections of the little thick spot from her brown age.

 Born in the Caribbean and raised in the U.S., **Tia Paul-Louis** began writing songs at age 11 then experimented with poetry during high school. She earned a BA in English/Creative Writing from the University of Florida along with a M.F.A in Creative Writing from National University in California. Her works have appeared in literary magazines such as *The Voices Project, Ethos Literary Journal,* and *Rabbit Catastrophe Review*. Some of her favorite authors and poets include Langston Hughes, Emily Dickinson, Maya Angelou and Edgar Allan Poe. Apart from writing, Paul-Louis enjoys music, photography, acting and cooking, though she mostly finds herself and others through poetry. She currently is living in Europe.

One Dead, One Among the Living Dead in an Asylum

Roy Bentley

Based on a story told by my grandmother, Susan Bentley

When people or things vanish at Eastern State Hospital,
it invites comparisons to sleight of hand. Prestidigitation.
Something palmed or taken away, and not by angels.
Comfort Rage, my friend, was visiting from her wing.
The Colored Only Wing. She started coughing—
she was a lunger, and sick, but I thought her cough
a tubercular spasm like others she had every so often.
I waited. I was sure she'd start in breathing again.
But when she didn't, I went and found Eugene.
Eugene is what we call the Floorwalker. Someone

who watches over us. He switched on the overhead.
It hummed a small, pure version of the Song of Light.
Eugene stood over Comfort Rage and raised her wrist.
Said, She's gone. And the fluorescents flashed. Winked.
Like a shock had passed through the whining white tubes.
Like what we convert to after this hard life, is electricity.
Comfort would have said believing that wasn't crazy.
Like a fairy god mother, she'd show up if I wished.
Sundays, mostly. She would call out *Susan Bentley!*
I'd stop swaying. Traveling in my mind like I do.

In no time at all, they made sure she was "seen to"—
meaning a pair of colored men came with a stretcher.
To my bed. And lifted the top sheet with her in it.
The men carrying the stretcher were quiet. I knew
not to speak about that, the men being quiet, though
the undeclared swirls up and floats away like smoke.
Truth is, patients at Eastern know not to tell things.
Crazy things. This everyone knows. Like I know
when Comfort Rage left her body—*vanished*—
in the Whites Only Wing, lights flickered.

Harry Houdini Dangling Upside Down after Having Just Flung Off the Straitjacket

Roy Bentley

One hundred and fifty feet above a street, a writhing man
is linking risk and recovery, death and a version of rebirth.

Let's just admit it: it's the body he wants to dispense with.
Let's say this takes place in July in Brooklyn, a straitjacket

an American emblem of the menace of economic catastrophe.
He's earning $3750 a week. Chaplin has a signed photograph

in an office that reads *Houdini with a hawk on his shoulder*.
Now the straitjacket glides belt-side down, flutters once,

recalling the light off of falling feathers, wings in flight.
He has his arms out, having earned a big-gesture tada.

Whoever has retrieved the certified-authentic restraint
isn't letting go but tugging at this keepsake of history.

In the heat of summer Harry Houdini rights himself,
waves to come down to the job of being part god

but needing to be unconstrained long enough
for blood flow to return to an arm or a leg.

Roy Bentley, finalist for the Miller Williams prize for his book *Walking with Eve in the Loved City,* is the author of seven books of poetry; including, most recently, *American Loneliness* from Lost Horse Press, who is bringing out a new & selected in 2020. He has published poetry in *december, The Southern Review, New Letters, Crazyhorse, Shenandoah, Blackbird, Prairie Schooner,* and *Rattle* among others. Roy lives in Ohio.

Codicil
Joan Colby

It is no use to speak to the dead.
Their essence has returned to starshine
A thousand light years away
From our footsteps still making noise.

Only the Indians knew how
To go silently, how to take the feathers
Of the wild and adorn the headdress.

Only the old women could
Prepare the body the right way
Laving it so carefully you'd think
Once they were lovers.

Only connect means nothing
As the barber advances,
His insignia of blood running fresh
Down the stripper-pole..

Only linger. These are the decisions:
What the body means when you no longer
Walk in it. Gravestone or burial at sea.

If you are to be burnt
Have them store your ashes
In a willow-ware urn on the mantel
Where they hang the gaudy stockings.

Frogs

Joan Colby

Harbingers of what's happening, they sing
Their love songs early in the spring.
Wood and swamp echoing
With the arias of peepers, the deep
Basso profundo of the bulls.

Scientists warn us that frogs
Are being feminized. Intersex
Amphibians infected by atrazine.
Herbicide goddess of the corn.
Here in the heartland, we don't drink
From our shallow or deep wells. Bottled water
From faraway springs is delivered
Like pamphlets from a shrine of purity.

The EU banned atrazine in 2003. When we turned
A cornfield into pasture, it took two years
For the soil to accept alfalfa and clover.
Meanwhile the frogs with inoperative ovaries
Are set for abolition
From the colony of the green.

We oversee field after field
After field—nothing but weedless corn,
That ordinary goddess of high fructose syrup
Hardening the arteries of our children.

Joan Colby has published widely in journals such as *Poetry, Atlanta Review, South Dakota Review, Gargoyle* and others. Awards include two Illinois Arts Council Literary Awards and an Illinois Arts Council Fellowship in Literature. She has published 21 books including *Selected Poems* from FutureCycle Press which received the 2013 FutureCycle Prize and *Ribcage* from Glass Lyre Press which has been awarded the 2015 Kithara Book Prize. Her newest books are *Carnival* from FutureCycle Press, *The Seven Heavenly Virtues* from Kelsay Books and *Her Heartsongs* from Presa Press. Colby is a senior editor of FutureCycle Press and an associate editor of *Good Works Review*.
Website: www.joancolby.com. Facebook: Joan Colby. Twitter: poetjm.

Snow in New York

Matthew Brennan

in memory of my younger brother Mike

The night I arrived we reminisced till twelve,
and then I slept the deep, long sleep of death—
until the metal scrape on pavement woke
me at three, the room brightened by white,
a quiet, opal otherworldly glow.

Later, in darkness, you rose up to brave
the long commute to get your chemo treatment.
But ice encased the car, like a great glacier
never thawed. You struck and clawed and quarreled
with the cold, stony block, a sculptor scorned
by his hard-hearted muse,
                              then marched us across
the snowy sidewalks to the subway station,
winded in the cutting air but charging
ahead of me whose longest steps kept me
almost behind you.
                        The train ferried us
beneath the buried streets and under the Hudson
to NYU. I watched you doze and held
back tears when Doctor Gu announced, "Six months
and then we need another miracle."
Outside, the buildings scraped the frozen clouds.

You beat the odds, but summer never lasts.
It's winter once again, and snowing in
New York. And though you've since transformed to powder
like night's first falling flakes, you're still ahead
of me, who's following in your footprints.

Migrant Geese
Matthew Brennan

I'm on the patio, gazing across
the street at a man-made pond, where a goose
has roosted. Her long slender neck extends
and nestles the new feathers of her spawn.

They float on the effluvia of sewage
spouting from a concrete hatch. Near dawn,
awakened from a dream, I look for them:

they're gone, but streetlights linger on the water,
a ghostly gaggle white as quarter moons.

Matthew Brennan has published five books of poetry, most recently *One Life (*Lamar U. Literary Press, 2016). A previous book, *The House with the Mansard Roof* (Backwaters Press, 2009), was a finalist for the Best Books of Indiana. Individual poems have appeared in *Tipton Poetry Journal, Notre Dame Review, Sewanee Review, Valparaiso Poetry Review, Poetry Ireland Review*, and elsewhere. In 2017, after 32 years of teaching literature and poetry writing at Indiana State University, he retired and moved with his wife and two cats to Columbus, Ohio.

Running on Water

William Greenway

for Betty

I dreamed again last night
that you could walk, taking
our hikes in Wales,
fishing from the shore in Florida.
And then you were even wading out,
and suddenly walking over the waves,
like Peter,
only no longer needing
a hand of help. And then,
not just walking, but running
over the blue-green sea,
and far below, making a new reef
for the fish, and a harbor
for your ship to come in at last,
your wheelchair.

William Greenway's *Selected Poems* was the Poetry Book of the Year Award winner from FutureCycle Pressand his tenth collection, *Everywhere at Once,* won the Poetry Book of the Year Award from the Ohio Library Association, as did his eigth collection Ascending Order. His publications include *Poetry, American Poetry Review, Southern Review, Missouri Review, Georgia Review, Southern Poetry Review, Prairie Schooner, Poetry Northwest,* and *Shenandoah.* He has won the Helen and Laura Krout Memorial Poetry Award, the Larry Levis Editors' Prize from *Missouri Review,* the Open Voice Poetry Award from *The Writer's Voice,* the State Street Press Chapbook Competition, an Ohio Arts Council Grant, an Academy of American Poets Prize, and been named Georgia Author of the Year. He is a Distinguished Professor of English Emeritus at Youngstown State University and now lives in Ephrata, Pennsylvania.

Animal Cracker Plan
Mark Weinrich

We were three mighty hunters
condemned to solitary in our
Dodge van. Our rations three
boxes of animal crackers and
a command to eat them slow.
For three boys from 5 to 9
this was our parents ingenious plan
to give them 20 or 30 minutes
shopping time and thus delay
inevitable fights. Of course we
committed outrageous crimes
against the animal kingdom,
until one of us claimed the lions
tasted better than zebras and zebras
better than elephants. Then
a cookie cannonade exploded
in the van, until one of us spotted
Mom and Dad. In a miraculous
union we debried all evidence of
our engagement. We were sitting
peacefully eating the remnants
of the shattered kingdom, hoping
that our parents thought their
plan had worked.

Mark Weinrich lives in Lubbock, Texas.

Law and Order

Jiahui Wu

angels in dissent
cannot ascend
get pulled back on the wings
tear
ask: why are we singled
out?
next to them
wheelbarrows
tilt
chicken hang
by their feet
their necks slit
and worms
rejoice
in the common
garden beds
there is no use working
angels
their noses ringed
are pulled
towards a mountain
top
where they are told:
you want
freedom?
from god?
must rid
you
of your malaise
angels
with wings clipped
are pushed off
the vast
and wide
mountain side
and fall
ten thousand

feet
reaching no bottom
devil catch them
laughing:
angels
look
what you've done?
is it not
nice
to be deceived?
I
all honest
you disbelieve
serve you right
to keep falling
for eternity!
angels bleed
cry
torn by crags
thorny creepers
meet the cries
of surprised critters
going about
their daily
chores:
look!
can you
believe?
there are
yet
   angels!

Jiahui Wu is a Hong-Kongese-Chinese-Australian visual artist and writer of poetry and fiction. She has published in various Australian literary magazines such as *Voiceworks, Cordite Poetry Review, Mascara Literary Review, Rabbit Poetry*, and so on. She currently resides in Adelaide, South Australia.

A Blue Collar Baby's Evening Prayer
A.C.Shields

Legend has it that a nightingale ensnarled in the thorns of a rose bush will sing out as they bleed to death.

They stood on porches and in front yards
crying out in hopes that the Lord
might be listening after all.
Their songs were all the same
sweet night birds weeping in the daylight
hoping someone will hear them chirping
and pull the rose thorns from their chests.
I felt their pain too realistically.
Bleary-eyed as I drive past the factory at night,
I have seen a village sink before.
I, too, cry out
but to the cold fescue behind chainlink fences
gripping fistfuls of dead grass and brown dirt in my hands
hoping the Lord might listen to me too.

A. C. Shields is an all-American radio news anchor and reporter by day and an unapologetic poetess by night. A Wisconsin baby who still winters with family in Marion and Indianapolis, Indiana, she is currently roasting in the deep-fried South with her two rescue pets, a composition notebook and her favorite blue pen.

Do Not Look Too Close
Erinn Batykefer

Your sight regenerates like a liver.

The eyelessness you endured
like a day lashed to rock has ended
on the sight of me

in Beltane's colors: dress silk like sky, throat roped
in pearls, dove-white, all of me lustrous as the air
after cloudburst.

But real time does not run as it does in myths and you know it.

Open your eyes. I am here, and impossible
Midsummer bounds the wood we walk:
lantern-strung trees, fierce heat, and maddened dancing—

a moment in this uncanny season could be a lifetime
of winters beyond, a lifetime healed and suspended
pre-dawn, before the coming birds.

Or, it could be a granted wish that you must pay for.
Look too close and love's glamour stretches thin.
Look at me, but do not look
at my eyes flashing carrion-bird yellow,

do not look at the dark shape of my shadow
lest you see how it trails from me
like a pair of wings.

Erinn Batykefer earned her MFA from the University of Wisconsin-Madison and is the author of Allegheny, Monongahela (Red Hen Press), The Artist's Library (Coffee House Press) and Epithalamia, winner of the 2019 Autumn House Press Chapbook Prize. She served as co-founder and editor of *The Library as Incubator Project* 2010-2017 for which she was named a Library Journal Mover and Shaker. She is an editorial assistant at *[PANK]* Magazine and lives in Pittsburgh, Pennsylvania.

Redefining borders
Bruce Levine

Dedicated to those
Who believe their own hyperbole
Rounding the edges with sandpaper
Emery boards of diamond dust
Redefining borders
Ignoring innate apprehensions of history
For the sake of their own place
In the sand-drifts of destiny
As Armageddon draws a line
Encampments of the disenfranchised
Awaiting the proximity of fate
Riding on the hyperbole of others

Bruce Levine, a 2019 Pushcart Prize Poetry Nominee, has spent his life as a writer of fiction and poetry and as a music and theatre professional. His literary catalogue includes four novels, short stories, humorous sketches, flash fiction, poetry, essays, articles and a screenplay. Nearly 150 of his works are published in over 25 on-line journals including *Ariel Chart, Friday Flash Fiction, Literally Stories*; over 30 print books including *Poetry Quarterly, Haiku Journal, Dual Coast Magazine*, and his shows have been produced in New York and around the country. His seven eBooks are available from Amazon.com. His work is dedicated to the loving memory of his late wife, Lydia Franklin. He lives in New York with his dog, Daisy. Visit him at www.brucelevine.com.

How My Father Became Irrational in Size
Hollie Dugas

We carried my father around for months
before his death. I could hear the whirlpool
inside his center when I embraced his fluid-filled
body against my ear, hauling him from room
to room as his skin stretched like ripe
black fruit. We lugged him like a sack of plums—

something doctors compared the size
of his growing cancer to, a single plum,

because it's too strange to carry grief alone.
As the end came closer, he called for me,
his butterfly, his voice like the metal lid of a jar
circling shut. He had wanted to continue
his work here as if he were a long-time
entomologist observing me skip from flower
to flower to touch something sweet.
Through the days, I watched him, how
he learned to become small enough to survive,
shrivel into a scar on my rib; how he came to be
irrational in size, easier to bear, camouflaged
in blankets. I, too, let myself slip into a cocoon.
I still don't wholly understand
that kind of backwards transformation— crawling
back into skin that has already been shed.
The morning of his death, I found a dead butterfly
on the front lawn, held it in my hands
and tried to place my naked faith onto its dark fruit-
colored wings, wondering from which god's
muddy boot it came.
My father bit down hard when he died—
Something's not right he said, gritting his teeth
as if he could create fire from the friction of bone,
willing to keep the connection to his failing body,
let it encase him like a heavy shell—a shelter
where we could both keep dreaming.

Hollie Dugas lives and teaches in New Mexico. Her work has been for *Barrow Street, Reed Magazine, Crab Creek Review, Pembroke, Potomac Review, Poet Lore, Watershed Review, Under the Gum Tree, Chiron Review,* and *CALYX*. Hollie has been a finalist twice for the Peseroff Prize at *Breakwater Review*, Greg Grummer Poetry Prize at *Phoebe,* Fugue's Annual Contest, and has received Honorable Mention in *Broad River Review.* Additionally, "A Woman's Confession #5,162" was selected as the winner of *Western Humanities Review* Mountain West Writers' Contest (2017). She is currently a member on the editorial board for *Off the Coast*.

Dream Catchers
Carol Hamilton

Two men I knew rode the rails
during the Depression. Begged then
because they had to but lived well after.
WWII explosives scarred one's hearing,
the other became alcoholic, divorced,
fought to sobriety and re-married his wife
when pain was left behind. Train whistles
are ghostly in the night, call out for a tug
at longing or remembrance, terror.
Some boys I knew jumped the trains
up from Guatemala and Mexico,
then lived in detention, mute
or missing limbs, in Harlingen.

Some friends I love lived
near the Verdigris River
and a hub of highways.
I lay awake in their old house
of Victorian vintage and listened
all night as long wailings cut
through night and memory.
Even without intention or ticket,
a train spells out travel,
dashes along bearing gang symbols
painted in stealth and memories
that stab out from its shrill cries.

Carol Hamilton has recent publications in *San Pedro River Review, Dryland, Pinyon, Commonweal, Southwestern American Literature, Adirondack Review, The Maynard, The Sea Letter, Tiny Spoon, U.S.1 Worksheet, Fire Poetry Review, Homestead Review, Shot Glass Journal, Poem, Haight Ashbury Poetry Journal, Sandy River Review, I-70 Review, Blue Unicorn, former people Journal, Poetica Review, Zingara Review,* and others. She has published 17 books: children's novels, legends and poetry. She is a former Poet Laureate of Oklahoma.

school dance
Abbie Hart

faces are made up
in ways they aren't usually
bodies are close
they don't want to be
it's got to be around 300 degrees
the music is so loud.
                              here is the scaffolding
                                  of a panic attack

everywhere i turn
there is someone
                          someone i did not want to see
then they are hugging me
and my vision is
the stop motion video
of a shitty phone camera
                                    pull it together.

                                   i am still upright.
                                    that's a start.

i am having a good time.
i am having anxiety.
                                my ex girlfriend spots me
                                from across the room
                                and moves to watch me
when i turn
she is gone.
nowhere to be seen.
                                she has her own friends
                                i tell myself.
my anxiety is gone too.
                                i am left to wonder
                              if maybe she was the source
                                    all along.
maybe she was the source
all along.

Abbie Hart is a 16-year old high school student in Houston, Texas. She has been published in *K'in Literary Journal* and is forthcoming in *Rise Up Review*.

The IRS Man Waits At Her Kitchen Table
Michael Jones

Returning without a scrap
of paper, she fills the kettle.
The twist she gives
the burner knob, betraying
no hint of her woodstove
childhood, arouses
in him an unfamiliar
uncertainty, as if she'd lit
a match and tossed it to him.

Matter
Michael Jones

My vertebrae
remind me I'm not
one piece, like this pebble,
but rather
assembled – which,
on second thought,
the pebble is, too:
a pueblo of particles.
Matter gives pleasure,
however peculiar,
like bending and
finding, in finding
rubble, articulate news
of being bound together.
a match and tossed it to him.

Michael Jones has taught in Oakland, California public schools since 1990. His poetry has appeared widely in journals (*Atlanta Review, Beloit Poetry Journal, Confrontation, DMQ Review,* etc.) and in a chapbook, *Moved* (Kattywompus, 2016).

The Day Before the Ultrasound Results
George Korolog

To consider death, one must be willing

    to stop asking why, to accept the utter futility

for instance, of raking leaves with three fingers

    or struggling for just one more breath because

everyone around you wants you to keep trying.

    In truth, to consider death, one must be willing

to forget everything and eagerly wash the dishes

    without reward, or scrub the counters with Clorox

to keep the ants out because that is life in the moment.

    To stare it down, you have to cut through it,

just like they're probably going to do once

    they get approval from the insurance company.

George Korolog is a San Francisco Bay Area poet and writer whose work has appeared in over 50 literary journals, including *The Los Angeles Review, The Southern Indiana Review, Rattle, Chiron Review, The Monarch Review, Naugatuck River Review, Word Riot, River Poets Journal* and many others. He has twice been nominated for the Pushcart Prize and twice nominated for Best of the Net. His first book of poetry, *Collapsing Outside the Box*, was published by Aldrich Press in November 2012, His second book of poems, *Raw String* was published in October, 2014 by Finishing Line Press. He is working on his third book of poems, *The Little Truth*.

Après Shankar
Karla Linn Merrifield

This long kiss
goes
on, on, on, and
on
like a sitar song—
a single chord relentlessly played,
for love
improvisational,
of exotic scale,
of timelessness.

Karla Linn Merrifield, , a nine-time Pushcart-Prize nominee and National Park Artist-in-Residence, has had 700+ poems appear in dozens of journals and anthologies. She has 14 books to her credit. Following her 2018 *Psyche's Scroll* (Poetry Box Select) is the newly released full-length book *Athabaskan Fractal: Poems of the Far North* from Cirque Press. *Her Godwit: Poems of Canada* (FootHills Publishing) received the Eiseman Award for Poetry. She is a frequent contributor to *The Songs of Eretz Poetry Review,* and assistant editor and poetry book reviewer emerita for *The Centrifugal Eye.* She lives in Florida.

The Earth Within
Michael Keshigian

We awoke in light,
wriggling in the palm
of a muddy hand,
divided into portions
under a stone,
we were the life
that delighted the sun
as we edged toward an empty cave.

Heaven rinsed us with a sigh
and set afloat
the Earth in our veins.
Behind our eyes
loomed the ocean,
beneath our fingernails
vegetables slept,
between our toes
hovered the path of discovery,
a model universe floated
undiscovered in our brain.
The great plates trembled
and the chatter of teeth
shattered the ensuing silence,
glacial ice masses cracked
and the capillaries of vision
slid into a sea of fascination,
a body born
under sunlight, in sand,
saturated with rain,
blossomed skyward
to propagate the world.

Michael Keshigian from New Hampshire, has been published in numerous national and international journals, recently including *Aji Magazine, Muddy River Review, Sierra Nevada Review, Oyez Review,* and *The Chiron Review* and has appeared as feature writer in over a twenty publications with 6 Pushcart Prize and 2 Best Of The Net nominations. (michaelkeshigian.com)

Too much time on my hands (and too little)
Gerard Sarnat

Long history of excess
chocolate, old-fashioned
or glazed French confections
with days left this calendar year,
I call my mail-order Medicare Rx
favorite tech to figure exactly how
to spend down to the round-off penny
$421.46 left before hitting that dreaded
donut hole so can stock chronic medicines
to treat high sugar/lipids/blood pressure/weight
plus stress so at least during upcoming holiday season,
our family won't need to see me having yet another heart attack.

Gerard Sarnat is a retired physician now living in California who has built and staffed homeless and prison clinics. He was also a Stanford professor and healthcare CEO. As a writer, he has won First Place in Poetry in the Arts Award, the Dorfman Prize, been nominated for a handful of recent Pushcart and Best of the Net Awards, published four collections and appeared in Stanford, Johns Hopkins, Harvard, Pomona, Brown, Columbia, Wesleyan, University of Chicago periodicals as well as *in Gargoyle, Main Street Rag, American Journal Poetry, Poetry Quarterly, New Delta Review, Brooklyn Review, LA Review, San Francisco Magazine,* and *The New York Times.*

The Women of Teheran
William Heath

Before landing in Teheran
one by one the women
remove their makeup,
put up their hair, hide
their leotards or miniskirts,
don black shapeless *chadors*.
Yet on the streets of the city
they stare in your face,
kohl shaping their eyes,
red lipstick, purple nails,
in spite of oppressive black.
Confronted with a camera,
they smile, sometimes pose.
At late-night private parties
they dress to the nines—
orange satin, heavy makeup,
luxuriant jewelry—dance
with abandon, flirt openly
with all comers. If Iran
is ever to break free of
the ayatollahs, these women
will surely lead the way.

William Heath has taught American literature and creative writing at Kenyon, Transylvania, Vassar, the University of Seville, and Mt. St. Mary's University, where the William Heath Award is given annually to the best student writer. He has published three novels, a book of poems, a work of history, and a collection of interviews with Robert Stone. His most recent chapbook is *Leaving Seville* from Persa Press. He now lives in Maryland. www.williamheathbooks.com

Small Town
Dave Malone

Starlings gloat in the street,
straddle mud puddles.

Gunslingers from spaghetti westerns,
the birds cock their wings
despite the city ordinance.

They shift their eyes, beaks,
to the rafters they've commandeered—
the bank, the drug store, the town café.

One of the city founders, a soft man
in an indigo suit, weeps. He thinks his fingers
still blue from the ink he signed with.

He recalls the mounds of orange earth,
so fresh like citrus, the bulldozers' hum,
more cicada than machine, until the lullaby ended,
until the lights opened the strip mall,
until the birds came.

I Bet Movie Actors Know This
Dave Malone

In memory, I'm doing things.
I know I drove that Datsun.
I bunked in a shack in the woods.
The Texas sun a red dart most days.
I hitched to Lubbock once
because the car failed me for the first time.
The Jemez girl found me in the truck stop.
She ferried me to a motel while the rain
sliced the gutters in half. On the balcony,
we held each other for an hour
or maybe ten minutes. I glimpse this now
in the mirror. But I'm not certain
it was me.

Dave Malone grew up in both Missouri and Kansas. He attended Ottawa University and later received a master's degree in English from Indiana State University where he studied poetry under Matthew Brennan. His most recent book is *You Know the Ones* (Golden Antelope Press, 2017). Works have appeared in *Elder Mountain: A Journal of Ozark Studies, San Pedro River Review,* and *Plainsongs.*

Last Word in an Argument Concerning Constellations

Casey Elizabeth Newbegin

You're angry with me
because I said
*You can't see Orion
in summer*; you've seen
him, you insist.

Once, when I was small,
a park ranger pointed
the white beam of his flash
light at the dark parking lot
pavement, chilled
August evening
star gazing, Devastated
Area Lassen National
Forest, when I asked
him where Orion was.

Tonight, we have
Aquila, Pegasus,
Sagittarius; what
you saw was just
any three stars.

Casey Elizabeth Newbegin lives and writes in Brooklyn, New York, where she works in art restoration. She has a BA in English from Lewis & Clark College and an MS in Information Studies from UT Austin. Her work has previously appeared in *Quiddity, Off the Coast, Argot Magazine, Grasslimb,* and *Windfall.*

The Wolf, The Falcon, and the Hawk
David Spicer

I drifted from the pack
when the other wolves ignored me
Your eyes they howled *your eyes
see things we can't your eyes lie*

I roamed these white mountains
under an expanse of blue everything
that never ended no matter how far
I explored and all I did was sing

Sing to the sad moon hunting
for its dark side
sing to lupine loners
who couldn't find wolves to love

I noticed the hawk before the falcon
she followed me from forest to forest
and I still see her on many nights
her fierce eyes tell me we are one

The falcon and I share the shunning
of our own kind who don't like our songs
but we sing to the beasts in the wild
in a language that few understand

I tell them I love each of them
in different ways like the loneliest tree
loves the snow or the way a new day
adores either rainfall or calm sea

David Spicer has published poems in *Gravel, Santa Clara Review, The Remington Review, Reed Magazine, Oddball Magazine, The Literary Nest, Synaeresis, Chiron Review, Ploughshares, The American Poetry Review*, and in the anthologies *Silent Voices: Recent American Poems on Nature, Homewords: A Book of Tennessee Writers, Perfect in Their Art: Poems on Boxing From Homer to Ali, Homeworks: A Book of Tennessee Writers* and *A Galaxy of Starfish: An Anthology of Modern Surrealism*. Nominated for a Best of the Net three times and a Pushcart twice, he is author of six chapbooks, the latest of which is *Tribe of Two* (Seven CirclePress). His second full-length collection of poems, *Waiting for the Needle Rain,* is now available from Hekate Publishing. His website is www.davidspicer76.com

Turtle Rock
Thomas Alan Orr

In the ditch along the field
a boulder, half-buried,
impedes the summer mowing.
It looms like a large leatherback turtle
in a sea of weeds, not moving
since the day a homesteader
cleared this land with a team of mules,
straining at their harness to drag it here.

Things block our way. We stub a toe,
stumble, step back, take a turn.
Sometimes we kick the rock,
enraged, until our senses numb
or we blunt the soul's keen edge.
The stone that dulls may also whet.
Yield without surrender. Resist with grace.

Thomas Alan Orr's most recent collection is *Tongue to the Anvil: New and Selected Poems* (Restoration Press). His work has appeared in numerous journals. He works for a community development organization in Indianapolis and lives on a small farm in Shelby County where he raises Flemish Giant rabbits.

A Writer's Fantasy
Patrick Kalahar

To capture the meanings between words
Visit the land of items lost on journeys
Touch wisdom and taste the sun
Circumnavigate the four corners of an empty room
Dance with angels on the head of a pin
And fly without regretting the ground
To live a thousand lives and
Be completely present in a single moment
Or paint the silence when the hawk nears
To stare at a blank piece of paper
And just one time
Know the truth—and write it

Patrick Kalahar is a used & rare bookseller in Elwood, Indiana with his wife, poet and novelist Jenny. He is a book restorer, collector, and avid reader. His poems have appeared in anthologies published by Poets Unite Worldwide.

My Son Takes His Daughter to the Synagogue
Michael H. Brownstein

My son and his wife go to the synagogue
The Friday before Rosh Hashana.
After days of heat and humidity, sun stroke,
Sweat, mosquitoes and giant horse flies,
Rain and then more rain, a cold rain, the grass
Slippery, the street a small stream and a pool.
Their three-month old baby lays in the car seat
And doesn't wonder what is going on
During the service. She is quiet and peaceful,
Attentive and thinking. This is now her world
And this is now their world. The Ark is opened,
The congregation rises, the congregation prays,
Bows at the right moment, sits when they are told,
And when the service ends, everyone--my son,
His wife, their baby girl--head to the backroom
For fresh bread and pastries, grapes and chocolate.
Outside it is still raining. Inside everything
Full of honey and the smile of the newborn
Bright as an evening star rising in the north.

Michael H. Brownstein's latest book, *A Slipknot Into Somewhere Else: A Poet's Journey To The Borderlands Of Dementia*, was recently published by Cholla Needles Press (2018). Michael lives in Jefferson City, Missouri.

Slippage

Richard Stuecker

Much of what was
seems to slip like warmth
over the jam under the door,
through the cracked window
we never look through
in the closet we leave
wearing new clothes.
I want to say:
That wasn't it,
it wasn't like that at all
no, not at all. Even
though you have the facts
like a game show contestant
or an entry in Wikipedia
or a poem filled with
clever lines that loses
its nuance in the cadence.
Even if I were to stuff
the jam with rags and
newsprint from yesterday
or glazed the forgotten window
still the sadness and emptiness
would stay while vivacity
through a mousehole would
find its way to slip out and away.

Richard Stuecker is a poet and writer who graduated from Duke University in 1970. A Pushcart Prize nominee, he is a student at the Bluegrass Writer's Studio MFA program at Eastern Kentucky University. His poems have appeared in or been accepted by *Tilde, Former People, Pegasus, Main Street Rag and District Lit;* creative nonfiction in *Hippocampus, Connotation Press, Brilliant Flash Fiction, Crambo, Louisville Magazine* and *Delmarva Review;* book reviews in the Louisville *Courier-Journal.*

Happy as a Clam
Gaby Bedetti

My son is a clam hidden below the sea.
    When the waves retreat, revealing the flats
along the coast, I attempt to rake him out
    with an invitation to the new action movie.

To find him, I look for a small hole in the sand.
    Alert to an air bubble surfacing, I offer
a bit of breaking news, or ask about the novel he's reading,
    and then dig gently before he retreats.

A rough tide or strong wind sends him
    deeper into the mud. If I unwittingly hit him
with my hoe, he won't bite, but he might squirt water
    as I try to winkle him out of his shell.

When he walks down the stairs to show me
    a text from his sister, I don't ask whether he needs
my car to go to the gym. In his room, my twentysomething
    is happy as a clam at high water.

Gaby Bedetti's recent poems have appeared in *Frogpond, Asses of Parnassus, Italian Americana,* and *Still: The Journal.* In June for the last six years, she has blogged a daily poem on https://lexpomo.com/. At Eastern Kentucky University, she teaches Comedy as an Artistic Approach, which culminates in public performance. Having translated Henri Meschonnic's prose in *Critical Inquiry* and *New Literary History,* she has begun to translate his poems from the French.

Sentencing
Don Kunz

When the sentence comes down,
You won't be plotting
White teeth and minty breath.
You won't be coveting
The new IPhone X
With two-way foldable case.
You won't be worrying about
Black Friday or Cyber Monday.

You'll be busy struggling to breathe
And hunting a warm embrace.
You'll be wondering how many steps
Your legs have left
When the sentence comes down.

Now imagine yourself at dusk
Across the street from a vacant lot
Considering how much ground
You need to hold what remains.
Wait to find yourself staring
Into a field filled with fireflies
Winking electric kaleidoscope gold
As darkness gathers around you.

Don Kunz taught literature, creative writing, and film studies at the University of Rhode Island for 36 years. His essays, poems, and short stories have appeared in over eighty literary journals. Don has retired to Bend, Oregon, where he writes fiction and poetry, volunteers, studies Spanish, and plays the Native American Flute. He is a member of The High Desert Poetry Cell, a group of five men who donate the proceeds from their readings and published books of poetry to non-profit community organizations.

The Body's Apocalypse
Katherine Hoerth

We call it an apocalypse—
Revelation, Armageddon, Ragnarok,
an ending of the world we know,
the moment when our existence ruptures
like time and space and darkness swallows
everything we love and everything we hate.

I stare at the CT scan on the monitor
as though it were map of stars up in the sky,
the aorta a path away from the heart,
the swelling sun above us all.
The doctor points to a black spot—
a tear in the fabric of the star dust
that makes up my flesh and yours
all things both holy and unholy.
It could erupt, at any time,
my own personal Vesuvius
hidden underneath a sheath of skin,
a bulging secret, mine to keep or tell.
I, like an Old Testament Prophet,
catch a glimpse of the final days
and know how the good book will end

but not the date. I imagine my heart a star,
burning brighter with every beat,
stretching the artery like the bounds of space.
We knew our world would end someday.

Katherine Hoerth is the author of three poetry collections, including *Goddess Wears Cowboy Boots,* which won the Helen C. Smith Prize for the best book of poetry in Texas in 2015. She is an Assistant Professor of English at Lamar University and serves as Editor-in-Chief of Lamar University Literary Press.

Girlfriend
Robert Hirschfield

When I took you
to visit her
(Yes, I know,
you don't exist.
Even now
you don't like it
when I hustle your molecules
into my poems about her.),
she'd ask over and over
like a black site interrogator
Are you Jewish?
Yes, you'd say,
lying for me.
When we got home,
I'd make love to you.
You didn't make love back.
You were moody and holy
like St. John of the Cross,
wanting only to burn
like an empty candle
inside me.

Mother The Fig
Robert Hirschfield

God, in his wisdom,
turned her into a fig.
Sometimes I'd see her
looking smug, chosen.
She'd tell the bank teller,
You are my father.
Jews in Queens
cleared a path for her
on the wide boulevard.
The fig is after all
the beloved of all God's fruit.
It was no surprise
when one day
she ate herself.

Robert Hirschfield lives in New York City. His work has appeared in *Salamander, Tears In The Fence, Tablet, Descant* and other publications.

omran daqneesh: the Syrian boy in the ambulance picture
Lou Ella Hickman

his face was on my news feed   how long ago
where
    he sits like an old tattered doll . . .
        his is the face of all the deserted, the defeated
        covered with the loneliness of desert dust
            his eyes are all the eyes that have known
                countless nights without stars
            his streaming tears are the tears of God weeping

for my sonnet: how to learn to speak to the deaf
Lou Ella Hickman

for all who have hearing difficulties

if you cannot sign
then be so spare
your words will be the light for their listening
speak   so that in every conversation you have with them
is a poem
a sonnet so beautiful shakespeare would weep if heard

Sister Lou Ella Hickman is a member of the Sisters of the Incarnate Word and Blessed Sacrament of Corpus Christi, Texas. She has a master's in theology and she taught on all levels, including college. She has worked in two libraries before working in a parish. Presently, she is a freelance writer as well as a certified spiritual director. Her poems and articles have been published in numerous magazines, including *After Shocks: Poetry of Recovery for Life-Shattering Events*, edited by Tom Lombardo, and in *Down the Dark River*, edited by Philip Kolin.

Regret

Lee Passarella

It is a photographic ghost.

It is the demimonde:
the shady, trick-
turning stepsister
of the day-lit hemisphere.

It is the demiurge:
the cosmic used car
salesman at the heart
of all that is quotidian.

It is the iceberg's
sunken hull
that unrigs each day's
most seaworthy constructs.

It is the hair shirt,
the millstone,
the one catholic
and apostolic jail.

Lee Passarella is a reviewer for *Audiophile Audition*, an online music magazine, and is a former senior literary editor for *Atlanta Review* and editor for *Kentucky Review*. His poetry has appeared in *Chelsea, Cream City Review, Louisville Review, The Formalist, Antietam Review, Journal of the American Medical Association, The Literary Review, The Wallace Stevens Journal, Cortland Review* and many others. He has published two young-adult novels, and his poetry books and chapbooks include *Swallowed up in Victory, Geometry of Loneliness, Sight-Reading Schumann, Redemption, Magnetic North* and *Ghosts and Illegals*. Lee lives in Georgia.

The Way Home
Mike Nierste

When my sleep was steady and deep
I found myself awake and alone with only him
peering out the windshield and back again
listening to stories between puffs of Pall Mall cigarettes
and the crinkle of cellophane.

We took a wrong turn.
Chicago was 115 miles away.
I was hoping there was no place to turn around,
that hours would be filled with stories of days gone by.
Hoping that this chance would yield some treasured time together.
That was the time before toxins inflaming rage,
before he could no longer break out of the Philip Morris cage
that trapped his heart
and lungs.
That was the time before eyes filled to flood stage.

Instead, we set our course
for a short way home and early good night
and agreed to turn off the lights.
Now sometimes I leave the lights
on at night because
I find myself awake and alone with only him.

Mike Nierste lives in Zionsville, Indiana and has been published in *Flying Island, frogpond,* and in the *anthology Cowboys & Cocktails: Poetry from the True Grit Saloon.*

Pickles
Mark Jackley

The last time I advertised on Match.com,
I actually gave some thought
to my marketing pitch.
"Looking for someone smart,
funny and possessed
of a warrantied BS meter."
That's how I met Kerstin.
A moment ago I was looking
for pickles in our fridge,
the ones I couldn't see
right in front of my nose.
"Male pattern blindness,"
Kerstin likes to call it.
I was looking for the big jar,
not this little one,
staring at a picture in my head. This is why
it has taken me
four wives to get it right.

Love
Mark Jackley

ark where two by two half hearts become one

Mark Jackley's work has appeared in *Fifth Wednesday, Sugarhouse Review, Talking River,* and other journals. His latest collection of poems, *On the Edge of a Very Small Town,* is available by emailing Mark at chineseplums@gmail.com. He lives in Purcellville, Virginia about 10 minutes from the Blue Ridge Mountains.

Driving the Grain

Cliff Saunders

One day everything can be fine.
The next day you come
tumbling down like a rock
on the edge of a black hole.

Are your prayers going
to make a difference?
It depends on how much
you can manage a flock of contrasts.

You're invited to provide
serenity, despite the typewriter
chained up like a dog.
The scariest thing you'll see

is an eye in the sky that works
too well. You'll see it
and a TV crew will capture it
and it'll be black

as a heart without a soul.
How will you ever come back
to life? You better not cry,
for liberty holds peace,

and the truth won't be blown
because it drives the grain
out of an English muffin,
because it's your elbow to the head.

Cliff Saunders is the author of several poetry chapbooks, including *Mapping the Asphalt Meadows* (Slipstream Publications) and *This Candescent World* (Runaway Spoon Press). His poems have appeared recently in *Atlanta Review, Pedestal Magazine, The Aurorean, Pinyon, San Pedro River Review, The Main Street Rag, Dream Noir,* and *Neon Garden*. He lives in Myrtle Beach, South Carolina.

Little Red Riding Hood: *A Memoir*
Ellie Dexter

I'm not little anymore: childbirth, motherhood, hips,
Honey-butter, salsa and chips. Sour cream.
But I was a knockout then.

None of the girls in the village liked me.
"If you ever run into a wolf that talks," they said
from under their drab capes, "Give him a chance."

I knew they were lying, but the idea seized me:
A talking beast? So, I set out in my riding costume.
I was a flame playing across the forest floor.

Oh, his eager lusty breath, to take off my hood and dress,
my anklets and shoes, the gauzy underwear
pressed upon me by the milliner's son.
To slide into my grandmother's sachet-laden bed with him to play
what-strong-arms-what-strong-legs what-white-teeth.

Now I'm a matron or at least matronly. I have children—
One a gymnast, one a soccer player, I drive a Toyota.
My husband still finds me desirable. I like it

When he slobbers, it reminds me of you-know-who.
Sometimes I think about the woodsman.
Without him I'd be dead.

But when I remember the wolf, snipped open like a pouch?
I cry and my husband stops what he is doing and kisses
My eyes. The better to see him with.

Ellie Dexter is a retired high school English teacher who lives and works on the New Hampshire seacoast. She writes in response to her life experiences using nature, the supernatural, and faith. She has previously published in *Tipton Poetry Journal*.

The Kitchen
Cary Barney

Diffident in death, you popped in,
a mute observer on irrelevant dreams,
out on the periphery, eying the exit.
Bored, you snuck away
before I could reach you.

Then one night you stayed.
We hugged in the kitchen as always
(when parents died, when towers fell),
clinging for dear life. You were warm, soft,
your hair black again. Back but still dead,
dead but still back. As you cleaned the kitchen,
soaking the dishrags in bleach, noticing
but not saying how I'd let things slide,
I told you how it's been, having you gone,
and you listened without replying.

I sank to the parquet hall floor,
my forehead touching it, and wept.
Relieved? Or knowing somehow
you weren't really there? You didn't
leave your cleaning to comfort me,
so my sobs became deliberate,
theatrical pleas for your attention.

Before I could know if they'd worked,
they woke me. Awake, I wept
a little more, then roused myself
to come and write it down,
relieved that I'm not over you,

that further down than words
I weep.

Cary Barney is an American expat living in Spain since 1991, a graduate of Marlboro College and the Yale School of Drama. He teaches writing and theater at Saint Louis University's Madrid campus. His poems have been published in *Third Wednesday, Quail Bell Review, Big WIndows Reivew,* and *Danse Macabre.*

New Hole
Jenny Kalahar

It appeared bottomless,
this new hole which gulped away grass and soil overnight,
but could have merely been a few feet in depth:
blackness looking the same either way

I kneeled before the pit
half wondering if it had completed growing
or if it was still slowly consuming my yard
and in so kneeling at the edge,
I knew I was secretly braver than I had suspected.
I shifted to press my whole body to the grass
trying to absorb vibrations
a seismic tremble
a growl from an unseen beast at the center of the Earth

The air from the hole was ripe
with the fragrances of a city reborn
a farm harvested
a white river flowing over blackgreen moss at its edges
scents of a glacier melting into ionized particles
lilacs withering into brownness
gravel roads
weedy lanes
bogs and byways
woods and asphalt
birch and pine
the sweat of tired children and animals
and the cast-off clothing of fishermen

I debated diving in
or jumping feet-first
or sliding into the everynothingness
to experience it all at once:
everything past and present,
all we were losing and gaining
and hurting and destroying and building
to get it over with in one blast of falling
in case this was it—
we were all to be eaten by holes outside our back doors
and this was my own, private hole
with my own, private blend of everynothingness
and each other person on the planet
had their hole waiting
for them to descend or avoid
much like the decision to go or stay
or yes or no
or never or now
faced every day
when startled eyes are first cracked open
away from dreams
away from other
unfamiliar holes

Jenny Kalahar is a used & rare bookseller in Elwood, Indiana, with her husband, Patrick. She is the author of ten books: novels, poetry, and short stories. She is the president of the Youth Poetry Society of Indiana, helms Last Stanza Poetry Association, and is working on the third novel in a series set in central Indiana. Her novel titled *The Great Restoration* involves the tent-show poets of a hundred years ago and Hoosier Poet James Whitcomb Riley.

in any given dream

Eugene Goldin

if it wasn't so high
up in the blue black
frigid sky
I'd be tempted
to hang onto
that spectacularly white
contrail

at least to do so
in any given dream

and while I would
I'd place my evening's catch
on clothes pins
along that white line
like fresh clothes
for all to see
what my heart
really looks like.

Eugene Goldin is a poet living in New York. His poems have been published in *The Poetry Quarterly, The American Aestheic,* and *The Fredericksburg Literary Review.*

The Spirit
Alessio Zanelli

A spirit dwells up there,
all over heights of endless glow.
I know the eerie place enough to speak,
but still I haven't found a proper name for it.

While roaming free on high,
the spirit holds me down below.
It seldom lets me rise above the dusk,
and when it does I wish I never had to quit.

Although the years rush by,
I hardly mind how fast they flow.
I'd rather research what the spirit is,
lest it may be my alter ego simply split.

Alessio Zanelli is an Italian poet who writes in English and whose work has appeared in over 150 journals from 15 countries. His fifth original collection, titled "The Secret Of Archery", was published in 2019 by Greenwich Exchange Publishing (London). For more information please visit www.alessiozanelli.it.

Gun Laws
John F. Buckley

Gun laws keep us safe. I snuggle
under the cloak of gun laws.
Gun laws keep Gabrielle Giffords safe.
The Second Amendment is a gun law.
Gun laws kept Christopher Michaels-Martinez safe,
for a while.
The Second Amendment prohibits King George III
from misappropriating Americans' military-grade ordnance.
Gun laws keep Jared Lee Loughner safe.

Safety is a precious commodity in the world of today,
like free-market Internet or extraordinary rendition.

Gun laws prevent me from wearing my assault rifle
in Chipotle, unless the Chipotle is in a church or a school.
Gun laws sometimes enable me to shoot skeet
in packed cafeterias.

My father hated gun laws.
My father loved gun laws.
Gun laws kept James Brady safe
as he accessed his special seat
at the Columbine Opera House.
My father still receives mail from groups
warning him that Barack Obama, Hillary Clinton,
and Nancy Pelosi still want to take our guns.
Then where will we be?
A totalitarian world without guns or laws,
a cross between Nazi Germany
and sheriffless Wild West towns.

If the Alpha Phi sorority had been armed
on May 23, 2014, they could have opened
the door to Elliot Rodger. In 2018,
the Census Bureau estimated
327 million people in the United States.
In 2017, the Small Arms Survey
estimated 393 million American
firearms in civilian possession.
Dad owned seventy-two guns at the time of his death.
Two thousand-plus pounds of powder in the basement.

Gun laws keep John Hinckley safe when he attends
midnight showings of *Taxi Driver* in Sandy Hook.

Gun laws are responsible for roughly thirty thousand deaths
in the United States per year. Two-thirds of them are suicides.
The rest are not.

Gun laws have enabled me to shoot
since I was four years old. Dad took us to the range
while Mom was at work. Due to gun laws,
Dad was able to cast his own bullets in the garage,
the wafting smell of molten lead interrupting
Saturday-morning cartoons.

Due to gun laws, since 1950,
every public mass shooting but one
in the United States has occurred in a place
where civilians are banned from carrying firearms.

Gun laws run rampant at gun shows across this great nation.
My father's gun laws were, "1. Safety. 2. Safety. 3. Safety.
4. Safety. 5. Safety. 6. Have fun. And 7. Safety."
He was the only NRA member I would trust with a gun.

Gun laws are intended to protect lives rather than take them.
So many gun laws.
So many lives.

Look at me, often a good guy, strolling through the mall,
openly carrying an AR-15 across my back.
My bandoliers are like suspenders.
They hold up a civil society.

John F. Buckley lives in Ann Arbor, Michigan. His publications include various poems, two chapbooks, the collection *Sky Sandwiches*, and with Martin Ott, *Poets' Guide to America* and *Yankee Broadcast Network*. His website is http://johnfbuckley.net. He's the fiction editor for the journal *Third Wednesday*.

The Nighthawks

John D. Groppe

Photo Credit: John D. Groppe

In the morning retirees gather here
in this clean, well lit place,
needing each other's jokes
and memories more than the coffee.
At noon, workers come for a quick lunch,
not for banter and memories.
After sunset come the nighthawks.
They sit apart, each to his own thoughts
of losses and what remains of hope.
The counter clerks,
busy at the drive up window,
leave them to their coffee
and will not notice that they have gone.

 **John D. Groppe's** *The Raid of the Grackles and Other Poems* was published in 2016 by Iroquois River Press. Mr. Groppe was listed on Indiana's bicentennial literary map *1816-2016 Literary Map of Indiana: 200 Years-200 Writers*. He is Professor Emeritus of English at Saint Joseph's College and a resident of Rensselaer, Indiana since 1962.

Bittersweet

Jeanine Stevens

There was a time I did love, as in dark things
...once: physical, forbidden,
no grammar, just lust under the crimson tupelo's

umbrella canopy or anywhere
in deep shadow:
shade of buildings,
billboards, gas stations,

pausing only to gulp down
a handful of salt tablets, necessary to cool.
I think of chocolate, espresso,
Sumatra, my deli sandwich: dark meat double-dipped.

You near the passageway: bare chested,
hematite pendant. Or was it the crypt with iron bars
preventing a twelve year old girl from entering.

Cemetery, noon sun alabaster on headstones,
more dangerous in late spring.
But often, just a place
for small blackbirds to rest in the slant of graves.

Driving on wet streets, clearing my head,
thinking of summer moths, birds in molt.

Jeanine Stevens is the author of "Limberlost" and "Inheritor" (Future Cycle Press). Her first poetry collection, "Sailing on Milkweed" was published by Cherry Grove Collections. Winner of the MacGuffin Poet Hunt, The Stockton Arts Commission Award, The Ekphrasis Prize and WOMR Cape Cod Community Radio National Poetry Award. "Brief Immensity", won the Finishing Line Press Open Chapbook Award. Jeanine recently received her sixth Pushcart Nomination. She participated in Literary Lectures sponsored by Poets and Writers. Work has appeared in North Dakota Review, Pearl, Stoneboat, Rosebud, Chiron Review, and Forge. Jeanine studied poetry at U.C. Davis and California State University, Sacramento.

*

Simon Perchik

It was a brook, had names
though these bottom stones
are still draining, passing you by

before letting go the silence
that stays after each hand opens
—you dead are always reaching out

—end over end unfolding your arms
the way each star ends its life alone
in the darkness it needs to move closer

become the light in every stone
as the morning that never turns back
keeps falling without any mourners.

Simon Perchik is an attorney whose poems have appeared in *Partisan Review, Forge, Poetry, Osiris, The New Yorker* and elsewhere. His most recent collection is *The Osiris Poems* published by *boxofchalk*, 2017. For more information including free e-books and his essay "Magic, Illusion and Other Realities" please visit his website at www.simonperchik.com. To view one of his interviews please follow this link:

https://www.youtube.com/watch?v=MSK774rtfx8

Night Landing, Kansas City
LuAnne Holladay

We break the cloud ceiling, shredding vapor,
aiming for ropy strands of light
and runways invisible, but apparent.

Thick with constellations,
the Solstice sky
has come to rest aground,
heavy with suburbs.

I'm a ghost in the window,
dropping foot by foot
from the ether,
braced to breach the vast dark ocean of 8 pm.

The middle-seat stranger beside me
is elbows knees and shoulders,
earbuds, iPhone.

He and I, together
in the night's reflection,
are brought low,
heavy bodies
meeting the rough scuff of land,
touching down,
touching

Lu Anne Holladay grew up in Georgia but lives in Indiana. She carves blocks for printing, manipulates and tests the limits of paper, and makes blank books, where all of her writing starts. Her short non-fiction has appeared in *Star 82 Review*.

To Foolishly Mount a Quiet Offense Against the Otherwise Insurmountable
Tyrel Kessinger

The ocean crawls from the conch shell and into my ear and makes a pulsing river of its ghosthiss. I have come to terms: we can only live for the moments in between, when life is good; time enough for the crust of the past to cool yet still warm enough for heaven to come down and live within you for a spell. When the river quiets and becomes a lake with a skirt aching to be pulled by a moon that hangs like an undecided coin. From beyond even that the blinkless starheat of Andromeda burns a hole in the lake's flimsy hide. The light goes only so deep before being lost, unable to pierce even this most simple of darknesses. If I throw a rock in, the peace will be disturbed. Or, even if I don't.

[This poem was first published in *The Inflectionist Review*]

Tyrel Kessinger is a stay-at-home dad of two wild animals. Occasionally, he finds time to write things, some of which can be found at *Gargoyle, Triggerfish Critical Review, Toasted Cheese,* and forthcoming from *SLANT* and *Straylight Magazine*. He also serves time as Poetry Editor for *Great Lakes Review*. He lives in Louisville, Kentucky.

Review: Creation Story by Steven Owen Shields
Reviewed by Barry Harris

Title: Creation Story

Author: Steven Owen Shields

Publication Date: May 1, 2019
Publisher: Brick Road Poetry Press

Steven Owen Shields' *Creation Story,* explores — often as funny or sarcastic creations themselves — just what it means to create: a universe, a multiverse, a planet, a donut, or a simple life on this earth.

As one begins reading, it soon becomes clear that this collection is veering away from most expectations a reader might extract only from the title. Though sprinkled with angels and spiritual themes and even biblical characters, this is no mere bible story.

The opening poem, "Dust Particles Suspended in a Ray of Light," poses its question: "Who is to say it does not happen like this?" A boy with a Polaroid camera takes a snapshot in a dusty attic just as a ray of light bursts through a window. The Polaroid photo captures small floating worlds suspended in time illuminated by the golden sunlight. His mother tapes the polaroid to the refrigerator and asks her son for a caption. The boy declares it to be "The Universe."

In the prose poem "Bang," an alarmed father scolds a son for creating the Big Bang.

> ... You *know* you're not supposed to be messing around with this stuff! And certainly not for something as small-ball as a fifth-grade science project. Do you have any idea what you've just DONE? This isn't some joke, mister; that Big Bang could have killed you, me, your mother AND burned down most of the neighborhood! Worse, now there are LIVING BEINGS in there we're going to have to think about and take care of for a long, l-o-n-g time.

While there are a good number prose poems in *Creation Story*, especially for the humorous narratives, the author sprinkles in a few *abab* arrangments, a sonnet about a chicken named Freckles who muses about the meaning of existence, and the villanelle "Stillborn."

Shields has organized his book into three sections: *Gnosis, Mythos, and Ellegia*. In the first *Gnosis* section, the legend of Yaldabaoth and Pistis Sofia from Gnostic literature is reframed in the poem "Donuts" as the demiurge Yaldabaoth (in this retelling as yet another young boy with an urge for wild creation) has created a silver platter of donuts — each a separate universe. His mother Sofia rebukes him:

> "You know what the Big Deal is, mister," she intoned. "Your father told you not six days ago to stop all this universe-creation nonsense. It just makes more work for him to un-do and frankly he's had just about enough of it."

All creation supposedly comes to an end one day. Shields portrays this in a prose poem, "The End of the Universe, as Told by the Building Inspector." The universe, in this case, is an abandoned dump "those investors from Fort Wayne thought they were going to front for the Chinese and make a mint. Never happened, of course." In fact it sat there, the building inspector says flipping through pages of documentation, for 28 billion years. Finally it's time for demolition:

> So then the demolition guys go in there and do their thing, wiring up the supports with the plastics, all the while not realizing there was one room that got missed somehow that still had a guy lurking in it. Can you believe that?! The bulldozers eventually spotted him, but not until after the fact. It was too bad but, you know, he shouldn't have been in there in the first place. Let me tell you, I wish I could have seen the look on HIS face when the blast happened.

In "On a Hillside Near Wapakoneta," Jesus comes forth from the clouds and looks around at the hillside populated by thousands of robots. Jesus asks *What have you done with my people?* The lead robot tells Jesus the humans were merged millennia ago. "Some of them are still within and among us, others of us have self-replicated according to binary theory, our Basic Law. It made logical sense to do so. ... After all, their mechanics were quite inferior." Jesus wades into the crowd "touching each and every one of them. And made the Word flesh."

The humor is never far away during the *Mythos* section. There are titles like "She Has Her Arm around the Man in the Moon," "The Martians Wore Bow Ties," "Young Tom Takes a Seat at a Bar in Downtown Appleton, Wisconsin," "Of Clockwork Elves, Illuminati, Aliens and Walt Whitman," and "Everybody Talks About Their Phantom Limb But No One Does Anything about It." My favorite poem in this section is "I Am Ten," 15 dispatches from a ten year-old mind posting thoughts about possibility like "if time is an arrow, what is the target?" and "If God could create a universe, what else could He create?" and pondering what would happen if he split his conscious from his unconscious. Would it float away? He defies gravity by jumping off the roof of his house wearing only underwear and a blanket. He forms a Unified Field Theory while he sleeps but by morning can no longer remember it. The last three dispatches are:

> 13. I am ten. I am also 10,000 years old. At least.
> 14. And I am no longer alone.
> 15.

The final section, *Elegia*, is about death or, more accurately, a lament for the dead. Sometimes the dead are real people, often friends or ancestors of the author. Other times the laments are more metaphoric or cosmic, such as "Death of the Sun" and "The Numbers of the Beast." One poem, "Blood Curse" about the 1930 lynching in Marion, Indiana on the courthouse lawn. The final poem in *Creation Story*,"The Idea of the Next World as a Valentine for Many People," offers up hope as a parting gift. The poem opens finding God sitting in a nursery with scissors and glue engaged in making Valentines and teaching children in the nursery to let the Valentines go.

> And fluttering, depart the room in silent flight
> to glide toward the darkness whence they came,
> and, landing, reawaken in the mortal heart
> the knowledge of the realm that is to come.

Ω

Steven Owen Shields is a former all-night disc jockey and present-day college professor of mass communication. Originally from Indiana, Steven earned his MA in Journalism from Ball State University and his PhD in Mass COmmunication from the University of Wisconsin. Creation Story is his second full collection. His work has appeared in *Angle, Deronda Review, Lyric, Measure, Main Street Rag, Midwestern Gothic, Raintown Review, The Reach of Song, Sleet, Umbrella* and previously in *Tipton Poetry Journal*. He and his wife Janet live in Johns Creek, Georgia, a northern suburb of Atlanta.

Barry Harris is editor of the *Tipton Poetry Journal* and three anthologies by Brick Street Poetry, Inc. He has published one poetry collection, *Something At The Center*. Barry lives in Brownsburg, Indiana and is retired from Eli Lilly and Company. He is married and father of two grown sons.

Editor

Barry Harris is editor of the *Tipton Poetry Journal* and three anthologies by Brick Street Poetry: *Mapping the Muse: A Bicentennial Look at Indiana Poetry; Words and Other Wild Things* and *Cowboys & Cocktails:Poems from the True Grit Saloon*. He has published one poetry collection, *Something At The Center*.

Barry lives in Brownsburg, Indiana and is retired from Eli Lilly and Company. He is married and father of two grown sons.

His poetry has appeared in *Kentucky Review, Valparaiso Poetry Review, Grey Sparrow, Silk Road Review, Saint Ann's Review, Boston Literary Magazine, Night Train, Silver Birch Press, Flying Island, Awaken Consciousness, Writers' Bloc,* and *Red-Headed Stepchild*. One of his poems was on display at the National Museum of Sport and another is painted on a barn in Boone County, Indiana as part of Brick Street Poetry's Word Hunger public art project. His poems are also included in these anthologies: *From the Edge of the Prairie; Motif 3: All the Livelong Day;* and *Twin Muses: Art and Poetry*.

He graduated a long time ago with a major in English from Ball State University.

Contributor Biographies

David Artis, who provided the photograph for this issue's cover, grew up in Terre Haute, Indiana, graduated from Indiana State University, and is now a software engineer living in Maryland, with photography for a hobby.

Cary Barney is an American expat living in Spain since 1991, a graduate of Marlboro College and the Yale School of Drama. He teaches writing and theater at Saint Louis University's Madrid campus. His poems have been published in *Third Wednesday, Quail Bell Review, Big WIndows Reivew,* and *Danse Macabre.*

Erinn Batykefer earned her MFA from the University of Wisconsin-Madison and is the author of Allegheny, Monongahela (Red Hen Press), The Artist's Library (Coffee House Press) and Epithalamia, winner of the 2019 Autumn House Press Chapbook Prize. She served as co-founder and editor of *The Library as Incubator Project* 2010-2017 for which she was named a Library Journal Mover and Shaker. She is an editorial assistant at *[PANK]* Magazine and lives in Pittsburgh, Pennsylvania.

Gaby Bedetti's recent poems have appeared in *Frogpond, Asses of Parnassus, Italian Americana,* and *Still: The Journal.* In June for the last six years, she has blogged a daily poem on https://lexpomo.com/. At Eastern Kentucky University, she teaches Comedy as an Artistic Approach, which culminates in public performance. Having translated Henri Meschonnic's prose in *Critical Inquiry* and *New Literary History,* she has begun to translate his poems from the French.

Roy Bentley, finalist for the Miller Williams prize for his book *Walking with Eve in the Loved City,* is the author of seven books of poetry; including, most recently, *American Loneliness* from Lost Horse Press, who is bringing out a new & selected in 2020. He has published poetry in *december, The Southern Review, New Letters, Crazyhorse, Shenandoah, Blackbird, Prairie Schooner,* and *Rattle* among others. Roy lives in Ohio.

Michael H. Brownstein's latest book, *A Slipknot Into Somewhere Else: A Poet's Journey To The Borderlands Of Dementia,* was recently published by Cholla Needles Press (2018). Michael lives in Jefferson City, Missouri.

Matthew Brennan has published five books of poetry, most recently *One Life* (Lamar U. Literary Press, 2016). A previous book, *The House with the Mansard Roof* (Backwaters Press, 2009), was a finalist for the Best Books of Indiana. Individual poems have appeared in *Tipton Poetry Journal, Notre Dame Review, Sewanee Review, Valparaiso Poetry Review, Poetry Ireland Review,* and elsewhere. In 2017, after 32 years of teaching literature and poetry writing at Indiana State University, he retired and moved with his wife and two cats to Columbus, Ohio.

John F. Buckley lives in Ann Arbor, Michigan. His publications include various poems, two chapbooks, the collection *Sky Sandwiches,* and with Martin Ott, *Poets' Guide to America* and *Yankee Broadcast Network.* His website is http://johnfbuckley.net. He's the fiction editor for the journal *Third Wednesday.*

Joan Colby has published widely in journals such as *Poetry, Atlanta Review, South Dakota Review, Gargoyle* and others. Awards include two Illinois Arts Council Literary Awards and an Illinois Arts Council Fellowship in Literature. She has published 21 books including *Selected Poems* from FutureCycle Press which received the 2013 FutureCycle Prize and *Ribcage* from Glass Lyre Press which has been awarded the 2015 Kithara Book Prize. Her newest books are *Carnival* from FutureCycle Press, *The Seven Heavenly Virtues* from Kelsay Books and *Her Heartsongs* from Presa Press. Colby is a senior editor of FutureCycle Press and an associate editor of *Good Works Review*.
Website: www.joancolby.com. Facebook: Joan Colby. Twitter: poetjm.

Holly Day's poetry has recently appeared in Asimov's Science Fiction, Grain, and The Tampa Review. Her newest poetry collections are In This Place, She Is Her Own (Vegetarian Alcoholic Press), A Wall to Protect Your Eyes (Pski's Porch Publishing), Folios of Dried Flowers and Pressed Birds (Cyberwit.net), Where We Went Wrong (Clare Songbirds Publishing), Into the Cracks (Golden Antelope Press), and Cross Referencing a Book of Summer (Silver Bow Publishing).
Holly lives in Minneapolis.

Ellie Dexter is a retired high school English teacher who lives and works on the New Hampshire seacoast. She writes in response to her life experiences using nature, the supernatural, and faith. She has previously published in *Tipton Poetry Journal*.

Hollie Dugas lives and teaches in New Mexico. Her work has been for *Barrow Street, Reed Magazine, Crab Creek Review, Pembroke, Potomac Review, Poet Lore, Watershed Review, Under the Gum Tree, Chiron Review,* and *CALYX*. Hollie has been a finalist twice for the Peseroff Prize at *Breakwater Review*, Greg Grummer Poetry Prize at *Phoebe,* Fugue's Annual Contest, and has received Honorable Mention in *Broad River Review*. Additionally, "A Woman's Confession #5,162" was selected as the winner of *Western Humanities Review* Mountain West Writers' Contest (2017). She is currently a member on the editorial board for *Off the Coast*.

Eugene Goldin is a poet living in New York. His poems have been published in *The Poetry Quarterly, The American Aestheic,* and *The Fredericksburg Literary Review*.

William Greenway's *Selected Poems* was the Poetry Book of the Year Award winner from FutureCycle Pressand his tenth collection, *Everywhere at Once,* won the Poetry Book of the Year Award from the Ohio Library Association, as did his eigth collection Ascending Order. His publications include *Poetry, American Poetry Review, Southern Review, Missouri Review, Georgia Review, Southern Poetry Review, Prairie Schooner, Poetry Northwest,* and *Shenandoah*. He has won the Helen and Laura Krout Memorial Poetry Award, the Larry Levis Editors' Prize from *Missouri Review*, the Open Voice Poetry Award from *The Writer's Voice*, the State Street Press Chapbook Competition, an Ohio Arts Council Grant, an Academy of American Poets Prize, and been named Georgia Author of the Year. He is a Distinguished Professor of English Emeritus at Youngstown State University and now lives in Ephrata, Pennsylvania.

John D. Groppe's *The Raid of the Grackles and Other Poems* was published in 2016 by Iroquois River Press. Mr. Groppe was listed on Indiana's bicentennial literary map *1816-2016 Literary Map of Indiana: 200 Years-200 Writers*. He is Professor Emeritus of English at Saint Joseph's College and a resident of Rensselaer, Indiana since 1962.

Carol Hamilton has recent publications in *San Pedro River Review, Dryland, Pinyon, Commonweal, Southwestern American Literature, Adirondack Review, The Maynard, The Sea Letter, Tiny Spoon, U.S.1 Worksheet, Fire Poetry Review, Homestead Review, Shot Glass Journal, Poem, Haight Ashbury Poetry Journal, Sandy River Review, I-70 Review, Blue Unicorn, former people Journal, Poetica Review, Zingara Review,* and others. She has published 17 books: children's novels, legends and poetry. She is a former Poet Laureate of Oklahoma.

Jiaxin Hao is a high school senior in Beijing with a passion for writing. Her poetry has appeared in *Inkbeat Literary Journal* and *Bridge Ink*. She was a finalist for *The New York Times* editorial contest in 2019.

Abbie Hart is a 16-year old high school student in Houston, Texas. She has been published in *K'in Literary Journal* and is forthcoming in *Rise Up Review*.

William Heath has taught American literature and creative writing at Kenyon, Transylvania, Vassar, the University of Seville, and Mt. St. Mary's University, where the William Heath Award is given annually to the best student writer. He has published three novels, a book of poems, a work of history, and a collection of interviews with Robert Stone. His most recent chapbook is *Leaving Seville* from Persa Press. He now lives in Maryland. www.williamheathbooks.com

Sister Lou Ella Hickman is a member of the Sisters of the Incarnate Word and Blessed Sacrament of Corpus Christi, Texas. She has a master's in theology and she taught on all levels, including college. She has worked in two libraries before working in a parish. Presently, she is a freelance writer as well as a certified spiritual director. Her poems and articles have been published in numerous magazines, including *After Shocks: Poetry of Recovery for Life-Shattering Events*, edited by Tom Lombardo, and in *Down the Dark River*, edited by Philip Kolin.

Robert Hirschfield lives in New York City. His work has appeared in *Salamander, Tears In The Fence, Tablet, Descant* and other publications.

Katherine Hoerth is the author of three poetry collections, including *Goddess Wears Cowboy Boots,* which won the Helen C. Smith Prize for the best book of poetry in Texas in 2015. She is an Assistant Professor of English at Lamar University and serves as Editor-in-Chief of Lamar University Literary Press.

Lu Anne Holladay grew up in Georgia but lives in Indiana. She carves blocks for printing, manipulates and tests the limits of paper, and makes blank books, where all of her writing starts. Her short non-fiction has appeared in *Star 82 Review*.

Mark Jackley's work has appeared in *Fifth Wednesday, Sugarhouse Review, Talking River,* and other journals. His latest collection of poems, *On the Edge of a Very Small Town,* is available by emailing Mark at chineseplums@gmail.com. He lives in Purcellville, Virginia about 10 minutes from the Blue Ridge Mountains.

Michael Jones has taught in Oakland, California public schools since 1990. His poetry has appeared widely in journals (*Atlanta Review, Beloit Poetry Journal, Confrontation, DMQ Review,* etc.) and in a chapbook, *Moved* (Kattywompus, 2016).

Jenny Kalahar is a used & rare bookseller in Elwood, Indiana, with her husband, Patrick. She is the author of ten books: novels, poetry, and short stories. She is the president of the Youth Poetry Society of Indiana, helms Last Stanza Poetry Association, and is working on the third novel in a series set in central Indiana. Her novel titled *The Great Restoration* involves the tent-show poets of a hundred years ago and Hoosier Poet James Whitcomb Riley.

Patrick Kalahar is a used & rare bookseller in Elwood, Indiana with his wife, poet and novelist Jenny. He is a book restorer, collector, and avid reader. His poems have appeared in anthologies published by Poets Unite Worldwide.

Michael Keshigian from New Hampshire, has been published in numerous national and international journals, recently including *Aji Magazine, Muddy River Review, Sierra Nevada Review, Oyez Review,* and *The Chiron Review* and has appeared as feature writer in over a twenty publications with 6 Pushcart Prize and 2 Best Of The Net nominations. (michaelkeshigian.com)

Tyrel Kessinger is a stay-at-home dad of two wild animals. Occasionally, he finds time to write things, some of which can be found at *Gargoyle, Triggerfish Critical Review, Toasted Cheese,* and forthcoming from *SLANT* and *Straylight Magazine.* He also serves time as Poetry Editor for *Great Lakes Review.* He lives in Louisville, Kentucky.

George Korolog is a San Francisco Bay Area poet and writer whose work has appeared in over 50 literary journals, including *The Los Angeles Review, The Southern Indiana Review, Rattle, Chiron Review, The Monarch Review, Naugatuck River Review, Word Riot, River Poets Journal* and many others. He has twice been nominated for the Pushcart Prize and twice nominated for Best of the Net. His first book of poetry, *Collapsing Outside the Box,* was published by Aldrich Press in November 2012, His second book of poems, *Raw String* was published in October, 2014 by Finishing Line Press. He is working on his third book of poems, *The Little Truth.*

Don Kunz taught literature, creative writing, and film studies at the University of Rhode Island for 36 years. His essays, poems, and short stories have appeared in over eighty literary journals. Don has retired to Bend, Oregon, where he writes fiction and poetry, volunteers, studies Spanish, and plays the Native American Flute. He is a member of The High Desert Poetry Cell, a group of five men who donate the proceeds from their readings and published books of poetry to non-profit community organizations.

Bruce Levine, a 2019 Pushcart Prize Poetry Nominee, has spent his life as a writer of fiction and poetry and as a music and theatre professional. His literary catalogue includes four novels, short stories, humorous sketches, flash fiction, poetry, essays, articles and a screenplay. Nearly 150 of his works are published in over 25 on-line journals including *Ariel Chart, Friday Flash Fiction, Literally Stories*; over 30 print books including *Poetry Quarterly, Haiku Journal, Dual Coast Magazine*, and his shows have been produced in New York and around the country. His seven eBooks are available from Amazon.com. His work is dedicated to the loving memory of his late wife, Lydia Franklin. He lives in New York with his dog, Daisy. Visit him at www.brucelevine.com.

Dave Malone grew up in both Missouri and Kansas. He attended Ottawa University and later received a master's degree in English from Indiana State University where he studied poetry under Matthew Brennan. His most recent book is *You Know the Ones* (Golden Antelope Press, 2017). Works have appeared in *Elder Mountain: A Journal of Ozark Studies, San Pedro River Review*, and *Plainsongs*.

Karla Linn Merrifield, a nine-time Pushcart-Prize nominee and National Park Artist-in-Residence, has had 700+ poems appear in dozens of journals and anthologies. She has 14 books to her credit. Following her 2018 *Psyche's Scroll* (Poetry Box Select) is the newly released full-length book *Athabaskan Fractal: Poems of the Far North* from Cirque Press. *Her Godwit: Poems of Canada* (FootHills Publishing) received the Eiseman Award for Poetry. She is a frequent contributor to *The Songs of Eretz Poetry Review*, and assistant editor and poetry book reviewer emerita for *The Centrifugal Eye*. She lives in Florida.

Casey Elizabeth Newbegin lives and writes in Brooklyn, New York, where she works in art restoration. She has a BA in English from Lewis & Clark College and an MS in Information Studies from UT Austin. Her work has previously appeared in *Quiddity, Off the Coast, Argot Magazine, Grasslimb,* and *Windfall*.

Mike Nierste lives in Zionsville, Indiana and has been published in *Flying Island, frogpond,* and in the *anthology Cowboys & Cocktails: Poetry from the True Grit Saloon*.

Thomas Alan Orr's most recent collection is *Tongue to the Anvil: New and Selected Poems* (Restoration Press). His work has appeared in numerous journals. He works for a community development organization in Indianapolis and lives on a small farm in Shelby County where he raises Flemish Giant rabbits.

Lee Passarella is a reviewer for *Audiophile Audition*, an online music magazine, and is a former senior literary editor for *Atlanta Review* and editor for *Kentucky Review*. His poetry has appeared in *Chelsea, Cream City Review, Louisville Review, The Formalist, Antietam Review, Journal of the American Medical Association, The Literary Review, The Wallace Stevens Journal, Cortland Review* and many others. He has published two young-adult novels, and his poetry books and chapbooks include *Swallowed up in Victory, Geometry of Loneliness, Sight-Reading Schumann, Redemption, Magnetic North* and *Ghosts and Illegals*. Lee lives in Georgia.

Simon Perchik is an attorney whose poems have appeared in *Partisan Review, Forge, Poetry, Osiris, The New Yorker* and elsewhere. His most recent collection is *The Osiris Poems* published by *boxofchalk*, 2017. For more information including free e-books and his essay "Magic, Illusion and Other Realities" please visit his website at www.simonperchik.com. To view one of his interviews please follow this link: https://www.youtube.com/watch?v=MSK774rtfx8

Gerard Sarnat is a retired physician now living in California who has built and staffed homeless and prison clinics. He was also a Stanford professor and healthcare CEO. As a writer, he has won First Place in Poetry in the Arts Award, the Dorfman Prize, been nominated for a handful of recent Pushcart and Best of the Net Awards, published four collections and appeared in Stanford, Johns Hopkins, Harvard, Pomona, Brown, Columbia, Wesleyan, University of Chicago periodicals as well as *in Gargoyle, Main Street Rag, American Journal Poetry, Poetry Quarterly, New Delta Review, Brooklyn Review, LA Review, San Francisco Magazine,* and *The New York Times.*

Cliff Saunders is the author of several poetry chapbooks, including *Mapping the Asphalt Meadows* (Slipstream Publications) and *This Candescent World* (Runaway Spoon Press). His poems have appeared recently in *Atlanta Review, Pedestal Magazine, The Aurorean, Pinyon, San Pedro River Review, The Main Street Rag, Dream Noir,* and *Neon Garden.* He lives in Myrtle Beach, South Carolina.

A. C. Shields is an all-American radio news anchor and reporter by day and an unapologetic poetess by night. A Wisconsin baby who still winters with family in Marion and Indianapolis, Indiana, she is currently roasting in the deep-fried South with her two rescue pets, a composition notebook and her favorite blue pen.

David Spicer has published poems in *Gravel, Santa Clara Review, The Remington Review, Reed Magazine, Oddball Magazine, The Literary Nest, Synaeresis, Chiron Review, Ploughshares, The American Poetry Review,* and in the anthologies *Silent Voices: Recent American Poems on Nature, Homewords: A Book of Tennessee Writers, Perfect in Their Art: Poems on Boxing From Homer to Ali, Homeworks: A Book of Tennessee Writers* and *A Galaxy of Starfish: An Anthology of Modern Surrealism.* Nominated for a Best of the Net three times and a Pushcart twice, he is author of six chapbooks, the latest of which is *Tribe of Two* (Seven CirclePress). His second full-length collection of poems, *Waiting for the Needle Rain,* is now available from Hekate Publishing. His website is www.davidspicer76.com

Jeanine Stevens is the author of *Limberlost* and *Inheritor* (Future Cycle Press). Her first poetry collection, *Sailing on Milkweed* was published by Cherry Grove Collections. Winner of the MacGuffin Poet Hunt, The Stockton Arts Commission Award, The Ekphrasis Prize and WOMR Cape Cod Community Radio National Poetry Award. *Brief Immensity*, won the Finishing Line Press Open Chapbook Award. Jeanine recently received her sixth Pushcart Nomination. She participated in Literary Lectures sponsored by Poets and Writers. Work has appeared in *North Dakota Review, Pearl, Stoneboat, Rosebud, Chiron Review,* and *Forge.* Jeanine studied poetry at U.C. Davis and California State University, Sacramento.

Richard Stuecker is a poet and writer who graduated from Duke University in 1970. A Pushcart Prize nominee, he is a student at the Bluegrass Writer's Studio MFA program at Eastern Kentucky University. His poems have appeared in or been accepted by *Tilde, Former People, Pegasus, Main Street Rag and District Lit;* creative nonfiction in *Hippocampus, Connotation Press, Brilliant Flash Fiction, Crambo, Louisville Magazine* and *Delmarva Review;* book reviews in the Louisville *Courier-Journal.*

Mark Weinrich lives in Lubbock, Texas.

Jiahui Wu is a Hong-Kongese-Chinese-Australian visual artist and writer of poetry and fiction. She has published in various Australian literary magazines such as *Voiceworks, Cordite Poetry Review, Mascara Literary Review, Rabbit Poetry*, and so on. She currently resides in Adelaide, South Australia.

Alessio Zanelli is an Italian poet who writes in English and whose work has appeared in over 150 journals from 15 countries. His fifth original collection, titled "The Secret Of Archery", was published in 2019 by Greenwich Exchange Publishing (London). For more information please visit www.alessiozanelli.it.

Made in the USA
Columbia, SC
23 March 2020